10 Ready-to-Go

BOOK REPORT PROJECTS

by Rebekah Elmore and Michael Gravois

SCHOLASTIC
PROFESSIONAL BOOKS

New York Toronto London Auckland Sydney

*To my professors at Wheelock College for introducing
me to the joys of teaching.*
— R.E.

*To Charlotte, Wilbur, Joe, and Frank who helped me begin
my journey; to Mrs. Lyons for the introduction; and to
Stephen for his encouragement along the way.*
— M.G.

Designed by Liza Charlesworth for Grafica, Inc.
Cover design by Vincent Ceci
Cover photographs by Donnelly Marks
Interior photographs courtesy of the authors
Interior illustrations by Teresa Anderko

ISBN 0-590-31444-0

☆◎☆ CONTENTS ☆◎☆

☆ ◎ ☆ INTRODUCTION ☆ ◎ ☆

As fifth-grade teachers, we've found that our students were developmentally ready to respond to novels and nonfiction books using their higher-level thinking skills. Therefore, we began to develop projects that would challenge them to think critically about the books they were

reading. We kept in mind that we wanted the projects to be interesting, fun, hands-on, and meaningful. These projects incorporate creative writing skills and artistic and oral expression. Because all of the projects focus on several intelligences, they allow every child in our classes to be successful. After creating several projects we began to realize that other intermediate teachers might also have the need for more challenging activities for their students, so we put our ideas on paper. This book is the culmination of our efforts. We hope your students meet with as much success as our students have.

Students creating Filmstrip Book Reports

How to Use This Book

10 Ready-to-Go Book Report Projects is designed so that you can pick and choose the projects that best connect with your curriculum as well as your students' interests and abilities. While some of the projects relate to a specific genre, they can all be easily adapted to meet the needs of your classroom. In the *Selecting Books* section we've highlighted specific ideas for choosing books for each report.

A student presents her Filmstrip Book Report

We've tried to include just about everything your students will need to complete their book reports.

Each chapter includes:

⦿ **Notes to the Teacher**: Suggestions on how to best use the unit and detailed directions on how to create the projects.

⦿ **Requirements**: Detailed, easy-to-reproduce directions for students on how to organize and create each project.

⦿ **Graphic Organizers**: Forms for helping students to organize their thoughts before writing their final drafts.

⦿ **Templates**: Forms students use to create an attractive, well-organized final product which can then be displayed on classroom bulletin boards, school hallways, shelves, tables, or windows.

⦿ **Rubrics**: Evaluation tools that make it easier for you and your students to know what is expected of them. For students, rubrics provide a wonderful way to do self-evaluations. For teachers, rubrics offer a more objective means of evaluating students. They allow you to focus on one element of the project at a time.

⦿ **Activities to Extend Learning**: Ideas for enhancing your reading and writing program through activities related to the book reports.

Biography Book Report bulletin board

Newbery Book Reports on display

Scrapbook Book Report

NOTES TO THE TEACHER

Students Will Need Copies of:
◉ requirements (pages 9–10)
◉ rubric (page 11)
◉ graphic organizers (pages 12–14)
◉ template (page 15), 2 copies
   for each student

Important Tips:
Give each student five large sheets of construction paper to use as the scrapbook. If you have a binding machine, you should bind them together along the short side. Otherwise the students should design a binding to hold the sheets together.

HOW TO USE THIS UNIT

1. First, review the requirements and the rubric with students. You may want to do the activity Share Your Scrapbooks (page 8) before you begin this report project.

2. Next, have students read their chosen books.

3. Then, have students fill out their graphic organizers. You may have them complete individual sections of the graphic organizers for homework. Check to see that they are on the right track.

4. Finally, check students' rough drafts for the writing sections of this project at least one week before the final project is due.

Selecting Books

While this report project can be adapted to most genres of books, we have found that it works particularly well with Women's History Month, which is celebrated in March. We ask our students to choose a book by a female author that has a female as its main character.

Suggested Due Dates

In order to help students pace themselves, set due dates for the following short-term goals:

1. Book should be read by: _____
2. Graphic organizers should be finished by: _____
3. Rough draft is due by: _____
4. Final draft is due by: _____

Setting separate "mini" due dates for each of the graphic organizers and their accompanying rough draft will help less-organized students.

ACTIVITIES TO EXTEND LEARNING

Share Your Scrapbooks
Invite students to bring in their own scrapbooks and share them with the class. If students do not have their own scrapbooks, have them bring in items from home that they could put into a scrapbook. Give students suggested topics to think about (hobbies, things they collect, places they have visited, awards, club activities, and major events).

Picture Book
Read a picture book that has strong character development. Then discuss with the class what things the character in the picture book could put into his or her scrapbook. Have students work in pairs to create a page for the character's scrapbook. Students can share the finished product.

Changing and Growing
Discuss with your students the ways in which people are always changing and growing. Brainstorm a list of suggested ways people change and grow (e.g., socially, physically, academically, emotionally, etc.). Then use a graphic organizer like the one shown to help students organize their thoughts on how they have changed from last year to this year.

Students can use their completed graphic organizers to write an essay on how they have changed and grown in one year. Invite students to share their essays with the class and discuss.

HOW I'VE CHANGED

One Year Ago → Academically → Today
→ Emotionally →
→ Socially →
→ Physically →

Name _____

Scrapbook Book Report

This report will be a character study of the main character of your book, and it will take the form of a scrapbook. You are to create a scrapbook as if it were put together by the main character.

☑ Check off each requirement after you've completed it.

Requirements

☐ SCRAPBOOK COVER

The scrapbook cover should include the character's name, the title of the book, the author's name, and your name. Be creative as to how you incorporate each of these elements into the cover.

Illustrate the cover so it is a reflection of the main character who created it.

☐ JOURNAL ENTRY

Write a journal entry from the main character's point of view that gives a summary of the book. The journal entry should:

1. Be written in complete paragraphs
2. Include a brief description of the following: main character, setting, major events, and conclusion
3. Be written on a sheet of paper and stapled, glued, or taped into the scrapbook
4. Include a date that reflects the "date" the character wrote it

☐ PICTURES AND PHOTOGRAPHS

Five pictures or photographs should be included ("photos" can be drawn or cut out of magazines). They should illustrate each of the following:

1. The main character in a scene from the book
2. The character's family or friends
3. The main character's major accomplishment
4. The setting of the story
5. A picture of your choice

◉ Use the templates on student page 7 for your pictures. Paste the pictures throughout the scrapbook and include an explanation that describes what is shown in each.

☐ LETTER TO A FRIEND/LETTER FROM A FRIEND

Write two letters for this section. Put each letter into a separate envelope, address it to the appropriate character, and tape it into the scrapbook.

Letter 1

Write this letter from the main character's point of view and address it to a secondary character. In it, describe the main problem the main character faces in the story.

◉ Describe the problem in complete, detailed paragraphs.

Letter 2

Write this letter from the secondary character's point of view to the main character, and in it describe the solution to the main character's problem as it happened in the story.

◉ Describe the solution in complete, detailed paragraphs.

☐ SOUVENIRS AND MEMENTOS

Draw, create, collect, or find at least six souvenirs that the main character would have put into the scrapbook. These objects should reflect events in the story or important aspects of your character.

◉ Include an explanation next to each object describing its significance.

☐ DIARY ENTRY

Write a diary entry from the main character's point of view that reflects the main character's feelings about himself or herself.

◉ Be sure the entry includes how the character changed from the beginning of the story to the end.

◉ Write it on a sheet of paper and put it into the scrapbook.

Name _____

Scrapbook Book Report R U B R I C

1. The scrapbook cover includes the character's name, the title of the book, the author's name, and your name. It is creatively illustrated and reflective of the character who created it.

    10   9   8   7   6   5   4   3   2   1   0

2. The journal entry is written in the first person, includes a summary of the book, and uses complete paragraphs.

    10   9   8   7   6   5   4   3   2   1   0

3. The pictures/photographs are creative and detailed. They illustrate the five required categories. A complete sentence describes each picture.

    10   9   8   7   6   5   4   3   2   1   0

4. The letter written by the main character describes the problem in complete paragraphs. It is imaginative and descriptive.

    10   9   8   7   6   5   4   3   2   1   0

5. The letter written by the secondary character describes the solution in complete paragraphs. It is imaginative and descriptive.

    10   9   8   7   6   5   4   3   2   1   0

6. The souvenirs and mementos are creative, and they are representative of the character and the story. A complete sentence describes each object.

    10   9   8   7   6   5   4   3   2   1   0

7. The diary entry reflects the character's feelings about himself/herself, describes how the character changed throughout the story, and is written in the first person.

    10   9   8   7   6   5   4   3   2   1   0

8. Grammar and sentence structure are correct (no fragments or run-on sentences; verb tenses are correct).

    10   9   8   7   6   5   4   3   2   1   0

9. Spelling and punctuation are correct.

    10   9   8   7   6   5   4   3   2   1   0

10. The overall look of the scrapbook is creative and neat. The layout is carefully planned.

    10   9   8   7   6   5   4   3   2   1   0

Name _____

Scrapbook Book Report GRAPHIC ORGANIZERS

SCRAPBOOK COVER

Use the boxes below to help you plan your cover. Create thumbnail sketches of possible covers. Be sure to indicate where you will write the character's name, the book's title, the author's name, and your name.

JOURNAL ENTRY

Write notes in the spaces provided to help you organize your journal entry.

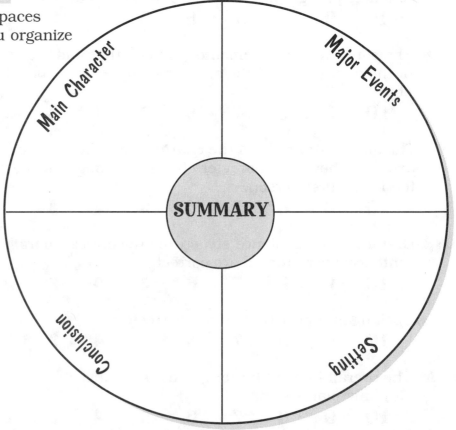

Name _____

Scrapbook Book Report GRAPHIC ORGANIZERS

PICTURES AND PHOTOGRAPHS

Draw some thumbnail sketches of what your pictures or photographs might look like.

The main character in a
scene from the book

The main character's family
or friends

The main character's major
accomplishment

The setting
of the story

A picture of
your choice

DIARY ENTRY

In the space on the left, describe how the character was at the start of the book. In the space on the right, describe how the character changed throughout the course of the story.

BEFORE	AFTER

Name _____

Scrapbook Book Report   GRAPHIC ORGANIZERS

SOUVENIRS AND MEMENTOS

Use the graphic organizer to help you brainstorm ideas for objects you might put into your scrapbook. Group your objects into categories. Two have been provided for you. Fill in the remaining categories yourself. List three objects under each heading.

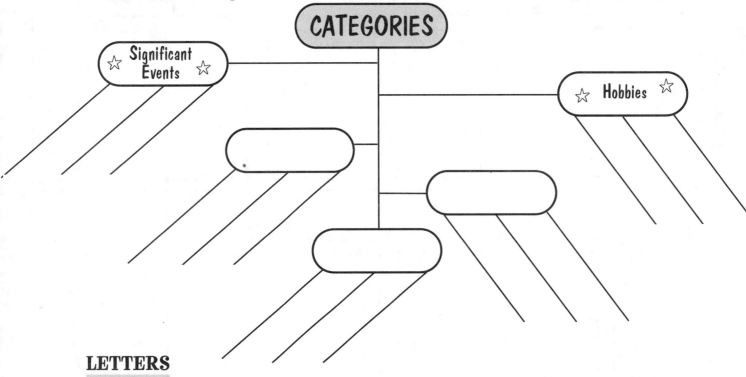

LETTERS

On the left side, write notes about the problem and ideas for Letter 1. On the right side, write notes about the solution and ideas for Letter 2.

LETTER 1: PROBLEM	LETTER 2: SOLUTION
The main character will write this.	*Which secondary character will write this?*

Name _____

Scrapbook Book Report T E M P L A T E

SCRAPBOOK BOOK REPORT PICTURES/PHOTOS

You may draw your pictures or photographs in the frames below, or you may create your own. After creating your pictures, cut out the frames and paste them into the scrapbook. Remember to write a complete sentence describing each picture.

Newspaper Book Report

NOTES TO THE TEACHER

Students Will Need Copies of:
- requirements (pages 18–19)
- rubric (page 20)
- graphic organizers (pages 21–23)
- templates (pages 24–27)

Important Tips:
The newspaper templates should be copied on separate sheets of paper so that students can choose the page order when constructing the final product. Students may need extra copies of the templates so they have enough room to write their articles.

HOW TO USE THIS UNIT

1. First, review the requirements and the rubric with students. You may want to do all or some of the activities on page 17 before beginning this project.

2. Next, have students read their chosen books.

3. Then, have the students fill out their graphic organizers. You may have them complete individual sections of the graphic organizers for homework. Check to see that they are on the right track.

4. Finally, check students' rough drafts for the writing sections of this project at least one week before the final project is due.

Selecting Books

We have used this unit during Black History Month, which is celebrated in February. In preparation for the Newspaper Book Report, we have our students read a novel by a black author or about a black family. However, you can adapt it to any theme.

Suggested Due Dates

In order to help students pace themselves, set due dates for the following short-term goals:

1. Book should be read by: _____
2. Graphic organizers should be finished by: _____
3. Rough draft is due by: _____
4. Final draft is due by: _____

Setting separate "mini" due dates for each of the graphic organizers and their accompanying rough draft will help less-organized students.

ACTIVITIES TO EXTEND LEARNING

The Five W's
Find a newspaper article related to your curriculum and make copies of it for each student. Ask students to find the *who, what, where, why,* and *when* in the article.

Analyzing Headlines
Have students bring in newspapers. Choose a headline in one of the newspapers and write it on the board. Review with the class the different parts of speech found in the headline and label them on the board.

Then invite students to work in pairs to find and cut out five more headlines. Have them write the parts of speech above each word in the headlines. Invite volunteers to share their samples with the class for analysis. Then discuss the following elements:

- lack of articles (*a, an, the*)
- use of fragmented sentences to highlight the main idea
- use of action verbs to grab readers' interest
- use of subheads when articles are continued on another page

Finally, pass out a copy of an article with the headline removed. Have students read the article and create a headline. Compare their suggestions with the actual headline.

Newspaper Study
Provide a newspaper for every two students in your classroom. Conduct a general discussion of the newspaper's format, layout, and sections. Focus on the following:

- how articles are continued on other pages
- editorials
- advice columns
- book reviews

Name _____

☆ Newspaper Book Report ☆

This book report takes the form of a newspaper. Use the following requirements to design and lay out your book report. Place the articles and features where you think they fit best.

☑ Check off each requirement after you've completed it.

Requirements

☐ TITLE/NAME OF NEWSPAPER

Create a title for your newspaper. It can be related to the book, your name, the class, your school, and so on.

ARTICLES

☐ Summary

At the top of the first page, write a summary of your book in a well-developed paragraph.

  1. Make sure your summary answers *who, what, where, why,* and *when.*
  2. Create a headline that relates to the summary.

☐ Main Character

Write a brief article about the main character.

  1. Describe who the character is, what he or she did, personality traits, and interesting things about the character.
  2. Create a headline that relates to the article.
  3. Draw a picture of your main character in a scene from the book.

☐ Antagonist

Write a brief article about the antagonist. Write in complete paragraphs.

  1. Explain why this person/thing is the antagonist.
  2. Create a headline that relates to the article.
  3. Draw a picture of your antagonist causing the problem.

☐ New Ending

Write a different ending to the book that changes the outcome of the story.

  ◉ Create a headline that relates to the article.

FEATURES

☐ Advice Column

Pretend the main character wrote a short letter to a newspaper advice columnist seeking advice about the major problem your character faces in the story. Create an assumed name for your character to use to sign his or her letter. Then write a response from the columnist that reflects how the problem was solved.

　◉ Make it look like an advice column.

☐ Book Review

Write a review for the book you read.

1. Explain your likes and dislikes.
2. To whom would you recommend this book? Why?
3. Create a headline for your book review.

☐ Editorial

Choose an issue related to your book and take a position on it.

1. Write a letter to the editor describing how you feel about the issue.
2. Think carefully and honestly about what you want to say.
3. Create a headline for the editorial.

☐ Comics

Design a four-panel comic strip that illustrates something funny that happened in the story.

1. Use the four squares provided.
2. Create a title for your strip.

☐ ADVERTISEMENTS, CROSSWORDS, AND MORE

All the space in your newspaper should be filled. After you have written all that is required, be creative to fill up the remaining spaces. Suggested possibilities include want ads, advertisements, crossword puzzles, word searches, riddles, or obituaries. Make sure they relate to the story you read.

Name _____

Newspaper Book Report RUBRIC

1. Your summary answers the five W's in a well-developed paragraph. Your headline is creatively connected to the article.

   10   9   8   7   6   5   4   3   2   1   0

2. Your article about the main character is written in a descriptive and insightful paragraph. Your headline is creatively connected to the article.

   10   9   8   7   6   5   4   3   2   1   0

3. The article about the antagonist is written in a complete paragraph. Your headline is creatively connected to the article.

   10   9   8   7   6   5   4   3   2   1   0

4. The problem and solution are creatively described using the format of an advice column.

   10   9   8   7   6   5   4   3   2   1   0

5. The new ending to your story is creative and changes the outcome of your story. Your headline is creatively connected to the article.

   10   9   8   7   6   5   4   3   2   1   0

6. The book review includes a good explanation of what you liked and disliked about your book. Your headline is creatively connected to the book review.

   10   9   8   7   6   5   4   3   2   1   0

7. Your editorial expresses an opinion and is insightful and well written. Your headline is creatively connected to your editorial.

   10   9   8   7   6   5   4   3   2   1   0

8. Your comic strip creatively illustrates a humorous event from the book.

   10   9   8   7   6   5   4   3   2   1   0

9. Spelling, grammar, and punctuation are correct.

   10   9   8   7   6   5   4   3   2   1   0

10. Rate visual presentation (writing, pictures, overall neatness, and use of all the space provided).

    10   9   8   7   6   5   4   3   2   1   0

Name _____

Newspaper Book Report GRAPHIC ORGANIZERS

SUMMARY

Write notes about the five W's to help you write your summary.

WHO ???	WHERE ???

WHAT ???	SUMMARY Headline:_____ _____ _____	WHY ???
	WHEN ???	

ANTAGONIST

In the ovals, list four reasons why this character is the antagonist. In the box, draw a sketch of the antagonist causing the problem. Use this information to help you write your article.

Antagonist's Name_____

Name _____

Newspaper Book Report GRAPHIC ORGANIZERS

MAIN CHARACTER

Fill in the data disk to help you write your article about the main character in your book.

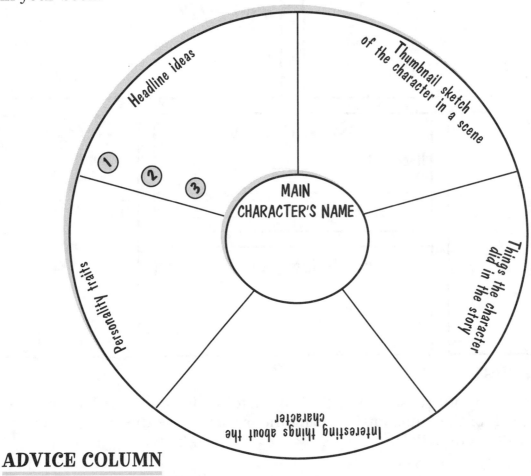

ADVICE COLUMN

Fill out the sequencing chart to help you write your advice column.

| List events that led to the problem. | Write notes about what the problem was. | List ways in which the problem was solved. | List ways in which the solution affected the rest of the story. |

Name _____

Newspaper Book Report GRAPHIC ORGANIZERS

NEW ENDING

Write notes to describe two possible new endings and outcomes to the story. Choose one to help you write your article.

New Ending 1	New Outcome 1

New Ending 2	New Outcome 2

BOOK REVIEW

List three things you liked about your book and three things you disliked to help write your review.

LIKED	DISLIKED

EDITORIAL

Choose an issue related to your book and take a position on it. List three reasons you might agree or disagree with your position.

AGREE	DISAGREE

COMICS

In the space provided, draw a thumbnail sketch of your comic strip. Include dialogue.

Title: ①	②	③	④

Name _____

Newspaper Book Report TEMPLATE

Vol. 1 No. 1	Editor_____	Date_____

_____
_____
_____
_____
_____
_____
_____
_____

_____
_____
_____
_____
_____
_____
_____
_____

Name _____

Newspaper Book Report TEMPLATE

Name _____

Newspaper Book Report TEMPLATE

Name _____

Newspaper Book Report TEMPLATE

_____

_____

_____

_____

_____

_____

_____

_____

_____

_____

_____

_____

_____

_____

Biography Book Report

NOTES TO THE TEACHER

Students Will Need Copies of:
- requirements (pages 30–31)
- rubric (page 32)
- graphic organizer (page 33)

Important Tips:
For this two-part report we ask students to create puppets as well as complete a written book report. You may want to suggest that students bring in extra cloth, buttons, and various craft items to share with the class.

HOW TO USE THIS UNIT

1. First, review the requirements and the rubric with students. You may want to do the Paragraph Sandwiches activity on page 29 before beginning.

2. Next, have students read their chosen books.

3. Ask students to fill out their graphic organizers. Check to see that they are on the right track.

4. Finally, check students' rough drafts for the writing portion of this project at least one week before the final project is due.

5. Because students are also required to construct a puppet and give an oral presentation, you should also hold a "mending and tending" conference to make sure the students are on schedule.

Selecting Books

We've suggested to our students that they do this book report project after reading the biography of any famous person. However, you may want to use this project to integrate other parts of your curriculum by having students read biographies related to other areas of study—for example, heroes of the American Revolution, inventors, explorers, and so on.

In order to help students pace themselves, set due dates for the following short-term goals:

1. Book should be read by: _____
2. Graphic organizers should be finished by: _____
3. Rough draft is due by: _____
4. Mending and tending conference will be held on: _____
5. Final draft is due by: _____
6. Oral presentation will be given on: _____

ACTIVITIES TO EXTEND LEARNING

Interview

Have your students interview an elderly relative (grandparent, aunt, etc.). Before they do the interview, as a class, brainstorm a list of questions that will help them gather information about the relative's history. After the interview have students use their answers to write a "mini" biography about the person they interviewed.

Autobiography

Have students write autobiographies. Begin by passing out index cards and telling them one card represents each year of their life. Students should put a number at the top of each card. (Card 1 will represent age one, card 2 age two, etc.) Brainstorm a list of ideas about what information they should gather about each year of their lives (e.g., where they lived, major events, friends, vacations, accomplishments, etc.). Suggest that students look through their baby books and family photo albums. Tell them to record the information they find on the appropriate index cards.

Family Tree

Encourage students to research their family's heritage (members, ethnic backgrounds, etc.) to design their own family tree. This activity works nicely as a follow-up to the autobiography and the interview activities. Have students create a graphic organizer to arrange their information.

Paragraph Sandwiches

Review the basic rules for writing paragraphs. Remind students of the elements of a good paragraph: topic sentence, detail sentences, and concluding sentence. It may help students to compare writing a paragraph to making a sandwich, the bread representing the sentences that frame the paragraph, and the meat, lettuce, tomato, and condiments representing the details (the "meat") of the paragraph.

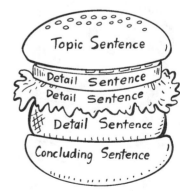

Name _____

☆Biography Book Report☆

For this project, you will write a report, create a puppet, and use your puppet to help you present your report orally to the class. Use the requirements that follow to complete your report and puppet.

☑ Check off each requirement after you've completed it.

Requirements

PART ONE: BOOK REPORT

☐ **Book Report Cover**
Create an interesting book cover for your Biography Book Report.

1. Include your name, the author, and the title of the book in an imaginative way.
2. Include a creative illustration that shows something important about your subject.
3. Use colored pencils, crayons, or markers for the cover.

☐ **Book Report Contents**
Your report should follow the format below:

First paragraph should include:

◉ The title, author, and a brief description of why the subject of the book is important.

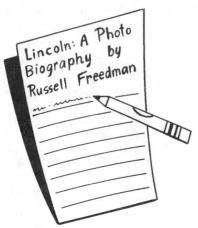

Middle paragraphs should include:

1. More details about why this person is famous.
2. Characteristics that helped make this person important.
3. Three things that made this person important.
4. Facts about how this person contributed to his or her field or specialty.
5. The part of this person's life you admire the most, and why you think so.

Concluding paragraph should include:

◉ A wrap-up of the body of the report. Include whether or not you think this book gives an honest account of your subject. Explain.

PART TWO: PUPPET AND ORAL REPORT

☐ **Puppet**

Create a puppet to represent your character.

1. Your puppet should be homemade using an assortment of craft materials. Be creative. Do not use any store-bought toys.

2. Have the puppet hold something that represents your subject.

☐ **Oral Report**

Prepare a three- to five-minute oral report on your subject.

1. Speak in the first person as if you were the character.

2. Use your puppet creatively during the oral report so it doesn't just sit there.

3. Be prepared to answer questions from the audience.

4. Have FUN!!!

Name _____

Biography Book Report R U B R I C

1. The book report is typed or neatly written.

   5 4 3 2 1 0

2. Book report cover is creative and has all required information (name, author, title, illustration).

   5 4 3 2 1 0

3. The book report follows the listed format.

   10 9 8 7 6 5 4 3 2 1 0

4. The book report includes all of the necessary information.

   10 9 8 7 6 5 4 3 2 1 0

5. Grammar, spelling, and punctuation are correct.

   10 9 8 7 6 5 4 3 2 1 0

6. Paragraphs are organized, detailed, and well developed.

   10 9 8 7 6 5 4 3 2 1 0

7. Puppet is creatively constructed using craft materials.

   20 19 18 17 16 15 14 13 12 11 10

8. Puppet looks like your famous person and is holding an object that represents him/her.

   5 4 3 2 1 0

9. You used the puppet imaginatively during oral presentation. The puppet did not just "sit" there.

   5 4 3 2 1 0

10. Oral presentation: spoke loudly, clearly, and slowly.

    5 4 3 2 1 0

11. Oral presentation: spoke in the first person.

    5 4 3 2 1 0

12. Oral presentation was informative and showed knowledge of the subject of the book.

    5 4 3 2 1 0

13. You listened attentively during other presentations.

    5 4 3 2 1 0

Name _____

Biography Book Report   GRAPHIC ORGANIZER

Important characteristics

1
2
3
4
5

SUBJECT NAME:

Reasons this person is famous

5
4
3
2
1

Important contributions

1
2
3
4
5

Experiences that made this person important

5
4
3
2
1

Things you admire about this person

1
2
3
4
5

Due Date:_____ Use this graphic organizer to help you organize your thoughts before you write your report. Complete the form using fragmented sentences and notes. ☆

Newbery Book Report

NOTES TO THE TEACHER

Students Will Need Copies of:
⦿ requirements (pages 37–39)
⦿ rubric (page 40)
⦿ templates (pages 41–43; one copy of page 11, six copies of page 42, four copies of page 43)

Important Tips:
If possible, copy the cover template on yellow or goldenrod paper. This will give the report the flavor of the Newbery Medal. Each student will need two brads to attach their reports.

HOW TO USE THIS UNIT

1. First, review the report templates and the rubric with students.

2. Next, have students read their chosen books.

3. Then, have students complete the rough drafts for each of the pages requiring writing. Check to see that they are on the right track.

Selecting Books

Beginning in 1922, a Newbery Medal has been awarded each year. A complete list of Newbery winners can be found on page 36. You may want to copy and display this list to help students choose books for their reports. Students can also choose Newbery Honor Books if they prefer.

--- *Suggested Due Dates* ---------------------------------

In order to help students pace themselves, set due dates for the following short-term goals:

1. Book should be read by: _____

2. Rough draft is due by: _____

3. Final draft is due by: _____

Setting separate mini-due dates for individual rough drafts will help less-organized students.

ACTIVITIES TO EXTEND LEARNING

Book Talk

Ask your school librarian to come in and discuss the history of the Newbery Medal, its significance, and why it was named after John Newbery. Have the librarian bring in samples of Newbery winners and honor books.

Dictionary Skills

This project asks students to alphabetically list and define ten words from the novel. You might want to review the rules for alphabetizing before beginning this project. You can also review the parts of a dictionary: guide words, pronunciation key, parts of speech, and so on.

Student-Written Sequels

Invite students to write a mini-sequel to their chosen Newbery book by placing the same character (or cast of characters) in a brand-new situation. Or, if students prefer, challenge them to create an alternative ending to the story. Remind children to think carefully about each character's personality and to try to generate plot lines that mesh with their characteristics and motivations.

Newbery Medal Winners

1922
Hendrik van Loon
The Story of Mankind

1923
Hugh Lofting
The Voyages of Dr. Doolittle

1924
Charles Hawes
The Dark Frigate

1925
Charles Finger
Tales From Silver Lands

1926
Arthur Chrisman
Shen of the Sea

1927
Will James
Smoky

1928
Dhan Mukerji
Gay-Neck

1929
Eric P. Kelly
The Trumpeter of Krakov

1930
Rachel Field
Hitty, Her First Hundred Years

1931
Elizabeth Coatsworth
The Cat Who Went to Heaven

1932
Laura Armer
Waterless Mountain

1933
Elizabeth Lewis
Young Fu of the Upper Yangtze

1934
Cornelia Meigs
Invincible Louisa

1935
Monica Shannon
Dobry

1936
Carol Ryrie Brink
Caddie Woodlawn

1937
Ruth Sawyer
Roller Skates

1938
Kate Seredy
The White Stag

1939
Elizabeth Enright
Thimble Summer

1940
James Daugherty
Daniel Boone

1941
Armstrong Perry
Call It Courage

1942
Walter D. Edmunds
The Matchlock Gun

1943
Elizabeth J. Gray
Adam of the Road

1944
Esther Forbes
Johnny Tremain

1945
Robert Lawson
Rabbit Hill

1946
Lois Lensky
Strawberry Girl

1947
Carolyn S. Bailey
Miss Hickory

1948
William Pene du Bois
The Twenty-One Balloons

1949
Marguerite Henry
King of the Wind

1950
Marguerite de Angeli
The Door in the Wall

1951
Elizabeth Yates
Amos Fortune, Free Man

1952
Eleanor Estes
Ginger Pye

1953
Ann Nolan Clark
Secret of the Andes

1954
Joseph Krumgold
And Now Miguel

1955
Meindert DeJong
The Wheel on the School

1956
Jean Lee Latham
Carry On, Mr. Bowditch

1957
Virginia Sorensen
Miracles on Maple Hill

1958
Harold Keith
Rifles for Waitie

1959
Elizabeth Speare
The Witch of Blackbird Pond

1960
Joseph Krumgold
Onion John

1961
Scott O'Dell
Island of the Blue Dolphins

1962
Elizabeth Speare
The Bronze Bow

1963
Madeleine L'Engle
A Wrinkle in Time

1964
Emily C. Neville
It's Like This, Cat

1965
Maia Wojciechowska
Shadow of a Bull

1966
Elizabeth Burton de Trevino
I, Juan de Pareja

1967
Irene Hunt
Up a Road Slowly

1968
E.L. Konigsburg
From the Mixed-up Files of Mrs. Basil E. Frankweiler

1969
Lloyd Alexander
The High King

1970
William Armstrong
Sounder

1971
Betsy Byars
The Summer of the Swans

1972
Robert C. O'Brian
Mrs. Frisby and the Rats of NIMH

1973
Jean C. George
Julie of the Wolves

1974
Paula Fox
The Slave Dancer

1975
Virginia Hamilton
M. C. Higgins, the Great

1976
Susan Cooper
The Grey King

1977
Mildred Taylor
Roll of Thunder, Hear My Cry

1978
Katherine Paterson
Bridge to Terabithia

1979
Ellen Raskin
The Westing Game

1980
Joan Blos
A Gathering of Days

1981
Katherine Paterson
Jacob Have I Loved

1982
Nancy Willard
A Visit to William Blake's Inn

1983
Cynthia Voight
Dicey's Song

1984
Beverly Cleary
Dear Mr. Henshaw

1985
Robin McKinley
The Hero and the Crown

1986
Patricia MacLachlan
Sarah Plain and Tall

1987
Sid Fleischman
The Whipping Boy

1988
Russell Freedman
Lincoln: A Photobiography

1989
Paula Fleischman
Joyful Noise: Poems for Two Voices

1990
Lois Lowry
Number the Stars

1991
Jerry Spinelli
Maniac Magee

1992
Cynthia Rylant
Missing May

1993
Phyllis Reynolds Naylor
Shiloh

1994
Lois Lowry
The Giver

1995
Sharon Creech
Walk Two Moons

1996
Karen Cushman
The Midwife's Apprentice

1997
E.L. Konigsburg
The View From Saturday

Name _____

☆ Newbery Book Report ☆

Use the templates and directions that follow to create a Newbery Book Report. After you finish the report, each page should be cut out, hole-punched on the asterisks (*), and fastened with two brads.

☑ Check off each requirement after you've completed it.

Requirements

☐ COVER
Use template 1. In the center of the medal write the name of the book and the author's name in a creative way. Also include your name at the bottom.

☐ PAGE 1
Use template 2 and label it: SUMMARY at the top. Then write a three- or four-paragraph summary of the book.

◎ **HINT:** Your summary should include a brief description of the following:

1. main characters
2. setting
3. major events
4. problem/ solution
5. conclusion

☐ PAGE 2
Use template 3 and label it: FAVORITE SCENE.

◎ Draw a picture of your favorite scene. Write a sentence describing the scene below it.

◎ **HINT:** Fill up all of the white space on the page with a colorful, detailed picture.

☐ PAGE 3
Use template 2 and label it: MAIN CHARACTER.

◎ Write a paragraph describing the main character. Tell how he or she changed throughout the course of the story.

◉ **HINT:** There are many ways in which a character can change throughout a story:

1. physically
2. emotionally
3. intellectually
4. spiritually
5. morally
6. maturationally
7. socially

◉ Think about these elements as you consider the ways in which your character might have changed.

☐ PAGE 4

Use template 3 and label it: IMPORTANT SCENE.

◉ Draw a picture of the main character in an important scene from the book. Write a sentence describing what is happening.

◉ **HINT:** Your sentences will be more vivid if you use descriptive adjectives and action verbs.

☐ PAGE 5

Use template 2 and label it: MAIN PROBLEM.

◉ Write a detailed paragraph about the main problem in the story. Write a second paragraph describing the solution.

◉ **HINT:** In the topic sentences for the two paragraphs, describe the problem or solution. Discuss the development of the problem or solution in the detail sentences. Summarize the main idea of the paragraphs in your concluding sentences.

☐ PAGE 6

Use template 3.

◉ Draw a line down the middle of it. Label the left half, PROBLEM and the right half SOLUTION. Then draw a picture of the main problem and solution in the story.

◉ **HINT:** It is a good idea to draw your pictures in pencil first and then outline them with black marker. Erase your pencil lines before coloring in the pictures.

☐ PAGE 7

Use template 2 and label it: ME AS A NEW CHARACTER.

◉ Then write a paragraph that answers the questions: If you yourself were a *new* character in the book, what would your role be? What would you have done in the story?

◉ HINT: You are creating a brand-new character, not using one that already exists in the story. Use your creative-thinking skills to write yourself into the story.

    1. Would your character change the outcome of the story?

    2. What is your relationship with other characters in the story?

    3. Are you a main character or a secondary character?

☐ PAGE 8

Use template 3 and label it: ME AS A NEW CHARACTER.

◉ Draw a picture of yourself in the story. Write a sentence describing what is happening.

◉ HINT: It is a good idea to draw several thumbnail sketches before working on your finished product. These sketches help you brainstorm ideas regarding the layout and design of your final drawing.

☐ PAGE 9

Use template 2 and label it: WHY THIS BOOK IS A WINNER.

◉ There must have been a good reason your book was a Newbery Medal Winner or Honor Book. What was it about your book that made it so outstanding? Write a complete and thoughtful paragraph. Cite specific examples from the book to support your feelings.

◉ HINT: Think carefully before answering this question. There are many elements that go into the selection of the Newbery winner. Brainstorm a list of ideas before writing your final draft. When citing examples from the book, include the page number on which the example can be found.

☐ PAGE 10

Use template 2 and label it: 10 NEW WORDS

◉ As you read your book, look up words whose meanings you don't know. List alphabetically 10 words that were unfamiliar to you when you first read the book plus their definitions.

Name _____

Newbery Book Report R U B R I C

1. The book report is written neatly in ink and in script, using my bes
   writing.
   10   9   8   7   6   5   4   3   2   1   0

2. The summary is detailed and accurate. It is written in three to fou
   plete paragraphs.
   10   9   8   7   6   5   4   3   2   1   0

3. The main character is described in a complete paragraph, and the paragraph also tells how he or she changed throughout the course of the story.
   10   9   8   7   6   5   4   3   2   1   0

4. The main problem and solution are described in two complete, detailed
   paragraphs.
   10   9   8   7   6   5   4   3   2   1   0

5. You have written yourself into the story in a creative and interesting way.
   10   9   8   7   6   5   4   3   2   1   0

6. You give reasons the book won a Newbery award in an insightful, thoughtful paragraph. You cite examples from the book and include the page num-
   bers on which examples can be found.
   10   9   8   7   6   5   4   3   2   1   0

7. The four pictures are detailed and creative. A complete sentence is used to
   describe each picture.

A. Picture of favorite scene	C. Pictures of problem and solution
5 4 3 2 1 0	**5 4 3 2 1 0**
B. Picture of important scene	D. Picture of yourself in a scene
5 4 3 2 1 0	**5 4 3 2 1 0**

8. Unfamiliar words are listed alphabetically and defined.
   10   9   8   7   6   5   4   3   2   1   0

9. Spelling, punctuation, and grammar are accurate.
   10   9   8   7   6   5   4   3   2   1   0

Name _____

Newbery Book Report T E M P L A T E 1

Use this for the cover.

JOHN · NEWBERY · MEDAL

Book Report By:

Name _____

Newbery Book Report TEMPLATE 2

Use this for pages 1, 3, 5, 7, 9, & 10.

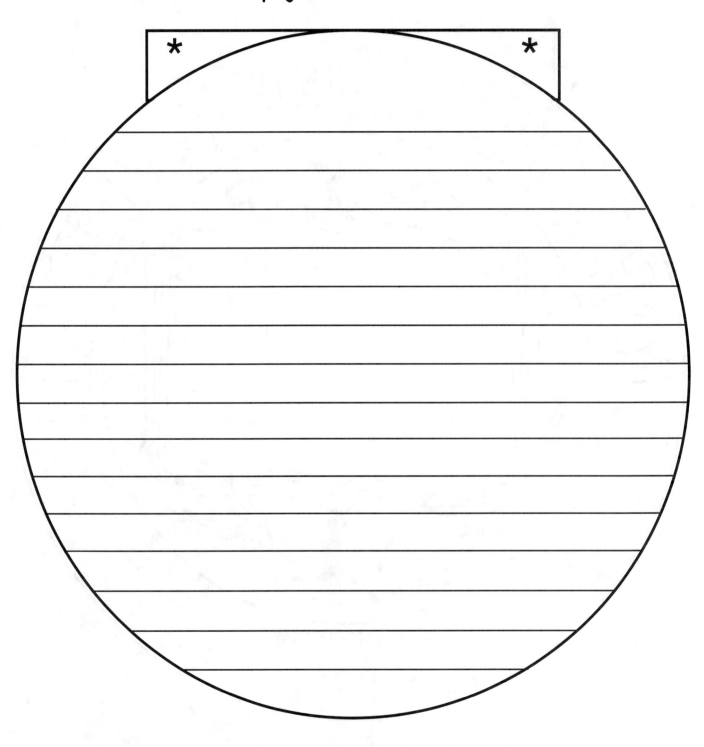

Name _____

Newbery Book Report TEMPLATE 3

Use this for pages 2, 4, 6, & 8.

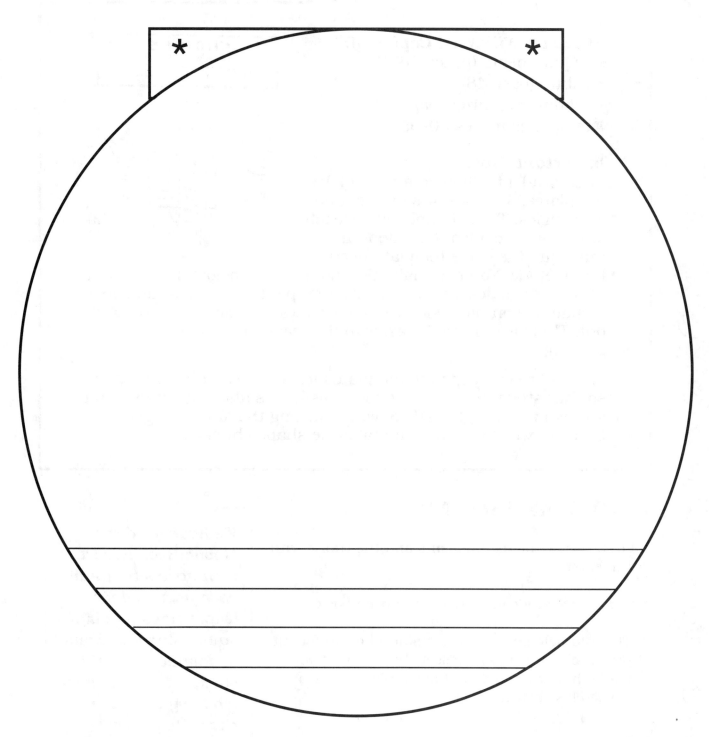

Mobile Book Report

NOTES TO THE TEACHER

Students Will Need Copies of:
- requirements (pages 46–47)
- rubric (page 48)
- graphic organizer (page 49)
- templates (pages 50–55)

Important Tips:
Each student will need a total of 12 templates: 4 circles, 4 squares, and 4 triangles. Three templates for each shape are provided; for side four, duplicate the same template used for side one. You can make the mobile more colorful by copying each of the sides on different-colored paper (i.e., print all copies of side one on blue, side three on red, side four on yellow, and so on). This also makes it easier to find each side when grading.

Make sure you copy the templates for side two onto white paper so that students can draw more easily. It's also a good idea to tell students to use glue sticks when putting the shapes together because wet glue tends to make the shapes buckle.

HOW TO USE THIS UNIT

1. First, review the requirements and the rubric with students.

2. Next, have students read their chosen books.

3. Then, to help students understand how to fill out the graphic organizers, select a choice that you made that day and fill out a sample form as a whole-class activity.

Selecting Books

We have used the Mobile Book Report with novels that have been assigned for whole-class reading so the students would be familiar with the choices/consequences made by the main character.

4. After that, have the students fill out their graphic organizers for the novel. We have students fill out the graphic organizers for homework, assigning each shape on a different night. Check to see that they are on the right track.

--- *Suggested Due Dates* ---

In order to help students pace themselves, set due dates for the following short-term goals:

1. Book should be read by: ____
2. Graphic organizers for the circles should be finished by: ____
3. Graphic organizer for the squares should be finished by: ____
4. Graphic organizer for the triangles should be finished by: ____
5. Rough draft is due by: ____
6. Final draft is due by: ____

Breaking up the report into three separate rough drafts—the circles, the squares, and the triangle—helps less-organized students.

ACTIVITIES TO EXTEND LEARNING

Choices and Consequences
Discuss with the class the fact that all choices have consequences. Some consequences are positive, some are negative, and some have elements of both. Show students how these consequences can be categorized into the following three groups.

COLOR	CONSEQUENCES
RED	**Lose/Lose** The choice leads only to negative consequences.
YELLOW	**Win/Lose** Some positive and some negative consequences result from the choice.
GREEN	**Win/Win** The choice leads only to positive consequences.

Ask volunteers to describe a choice that they made and the consequences of that choice. Decide which category the consequences fall into. Discuss alternative choices that the student could have made and how the consequences would have been affected. Recategorize these consequences.

Name _____

☆ Mobile Book Report ☆

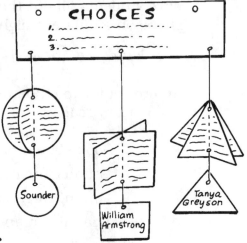

For this 3-D report, you need to choose three of the major choices that the main character made in the novel. For each choice, you will create a four-sided shape. Each side should correspond to the guidelines listed below. Use the templates provided for your final draft.

☑ Check off each requirement after you've completed it.

Requirements

☐ SIDE ONE

Pick one of the major choices that the main character made in the novel. Use one of the three shapes (circle, square, triangle). On side one write a complete, detailed paragraph describing the situation your character was in before making the choice, the choice that he or she made, and the consequence of that choice.

☐ SIDE TWO

On side two of that shape, draw a picture of the main character making the decision. Your drawing should illustrate the paragraph on side one.

1. All illustrations must be colored in with either markers, colored pencils, or crayons.
2. Outlining the drawings with black marker helps make the colors stand out.

☐ SIDE THREE

Draw a line down the middle of the shape. Label the left side: ALTERNATE CHOICES. Label the right side: CONSEQUENCES. Write the number 1 on the first line of both sides. Write the number 2 on both sides about 5 lines down. Then write the number 3 on both sides about 10 lines down.

1. Write three alternate choices that the main character could have made instead of the choice he or she did make.
2. Beside each choice, list the consequences that would have happened if that choice had been made. These consequences should be completely different from anything that happened in the story.
3. All of the choices and consequences should be written in complete sentences.

☐ SIDE FOUR

Select one of your three alternate choices/consequences from side three. Then write a new ending for your book using this choice and its consequences. Make sure your ending is written in a complete, detailed paragraph.

☐ CONSTRUCTION OF THE MOBILE

Find some rectangular-shaped corrugated cardboard and cover it neatly with construction paper or colorful paper. Use creative lettering to write the label CHOICES on both sides. Under the title, use complete sentences to write down the three major choices the main character made in the book. Add a decorative border.

3-D Shapes

Once you've finished with all four sides of one shape, cut them out and use a glue stick (not glue) to attach them as shown below. Repeat this process for all three shapes.

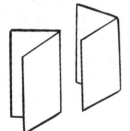 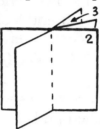 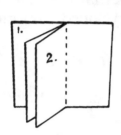 

1. Fold each shape lengthwise.

2. Attach side one to side two.

3. Attach side two to side three, etc.

4. The fourth side should be attached to side one, completing the 3-D shape.

Small Shapes

1. Cut out the smaller shapes on the template pages.

2. On both sides of the circle write the name of the book.

3. On both sides of the square write the author's name.

4. On both sides of the triangle write your name. Use creative lettering and decorate these shapes in an imaginative way.

Putting It Together

1. Punch three holes along the bottom of your cardboard frame.

2. Punch a hole in the top center of each 3-D shape.

3. Tie strings of different lengths from the cardboard frame to each shape.

4. Punch a hole in the bottom center of each 3-D shape.

5. Punch a hole at the top of each shape that has your name, the title, and the author's name.

6. Tie each of the small shapes to the larger ones.

7. Finally, punch two holes in the top of your cardboard frame and tie strings from each hole so the mobile can be hung in the classroom.

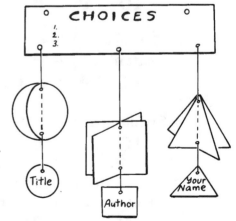

Name _____

Mobile Book Report R U B R I C

1. The construction of your mobile follows the guidelines listed on page two of the requirements. The overall look of the mobile is creative and neat. It is written in ink and in script using your best handwriting.

    10 9 8 7 6 5 4 3 2 1 0

2. The list of three choices on your cardboard frame are written in complete sentences. You used creative lettering for the title and the list of choices. You created a decorative border on both sides.

    10 9 8 7 6 5 4 3 2 1 0

3. The paragraphs about the three choices that the main character made in the book are clearly written and well developed. You included information about the situation and consequences.

    15 14 13 12 11 10 9 8 7 6 5 4 3 2 1 0

4. The pictures you drew are representative of the choices the character had to make. They are detailed and creative.

    10 9 8 7 6 5 4 3 2 1 0

5. You provided three creative alternatives for your character for each choice. Each choice is developed in a clear and complete sentence.

    10 9 8 7 6 5 4 3 2 1 0

6. You provided three sensible consequences for each alternate choice you made. Each consequence is directly connected to the choice you created and is written in clear, complete paragraphs.

    10 9 8 7 6 5 4 3 2 1 0

7. The new endings to your novel are creative, brief, and complete. They are written in well-developed paragraphs.

    15 14 13 12 11 10 9 8 7 6 5 4 3 2 1 0

8. Spelling, grammar, and punctuation are correct.

    10 9 8 7 6 5 4 3 2 1 0

9. Title, author's name, and your name are creatively executed and hang below each 3-D shape.

    10 9 8 7 6 5 4 3 2 1 0

Name _____

Mobile Book Report GRAPHIC ORGANIZERS

SHAPE

Side One: Pick one of the major choices that the main character made in the novel and fill out the flow chart.

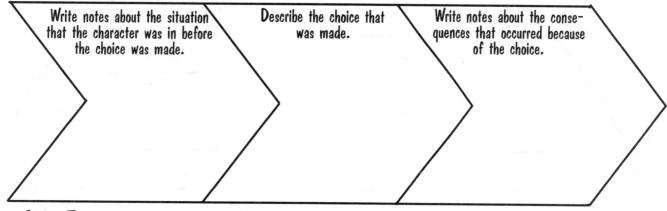

Write notes about the situation that the character was in before the choice was made.

Describe the choice that was made.

Write notes about the consequences that occurred because of the choice.

Side Two: On the back of this paper, draw three thumbnail sketches of the main character making the choice described above.

Side Three: Think about other options the main character could have chosen instead of the one listed above. Write notes about the alternate choices, and then describe the consequences that each choice would have had.

Option 1	Option 2	Option 3

Consequence 1	Consequence 2	Consequence 3

Side Four: Choose one of the options listed above and brainstorm a list of ideas for the new ending to your story. Use the back of this paper to write your new ideas.

Name _____

Mobile Book Report TEMPLATE

Use this for sides 1, 3, & 4.

Name _____

Mobile Book Report TEMPLATE

Use this for side 2.

Use this for title.

Name _____

Mobile Book Report TEMPLATE

Use this for sides 1, 3, & 4.

Name _____

Mobile Book Report TEMPLATE

Use this for side **2**.

Use this for author's name.

Name _____

Mobile Book Report TEMPLATE

Use this for sides 1, 3, & 4.

Name _____

Mobile Book Report TEMPLATE

Use this for
your name.

Use this for side 2.

Filmstrip Book Report

NOTES TO THE TEACHER

Students Will Need Copies of:
- requirements (pages 58–59)
- rubric (page 60)
- graphic organizers (pages 61–62)
- template (page 63); each student needs a total of nine panels— three three-panel strips

Important Tips:
This project makes a great display hanging on the classroom windows. Use clear tape to attach the filmstrips.

HOW TO USE THIS UNIT

1. First, review the requirements and the rubric with students.

2. Next, have students select three books related to a topic you are studying.

3. Then, review the books each student chose. Select one of the books for the student to read completely. Have them use the other two books for reference.

4. Have students fill out their graphic organizers. You may have them complete individual sections of the graphic organizers for homework. Check to see that they are on the right track.

5. Have students complete the black-and-white versions of their filmstrips.

6. Copy the filmstrips onto overhead transparencies.

Selecting Books

We have used this project for nonfiction science and social studies book reports, but it can easily be adapted for a variety of uses. You can have students research famous people associated with a topic you are studying, or students can use the project to report on an assigned section from a textbook.

7. Have the students use permanent markers to color in their filmstrips. They should color the *back* of the transparency so the black lines don't rub off.

8. Finally, create an "Oral Presentation Template" for your overhead projector. Cut out a rectangle (3.75 x 2.75 inches) in the middle of an 8.5-x-1-inch piece of paper. Tape this onto your overhead projector and have students pull their filmstrips across the template as they give their oral presentations.

Suggested Due Dates

In order to help students pace themselves, set due dates for the following short-term goals:

1. Decide upon topic and choose books by: _____
2. Book should be read by: _____
3. Graphic organizers should be finished by: _____
4. Black-and-white filmstrip is due by: _____
5. Color filmstrip is due by: _____
6. Oral presentations will be given on: _____

Breaking up the report into separate due dates helps less-organized students.

ACTIVITIES TO EXTEND LEARNING

Note Taking

Discuss with the class the importance of learning the skill of note taking. Notes help you recall information you have read and should include the main ideas and most important details about a subject. Give each student a copy of the passage from a textbook or newspaper. Have them read the passage and underline the main ideas and important details. Have them rewrite in note form the phrases they underline. Ask volunteers to read phrases they underlined and the corresponding note they wrote.

Writing a Bibliography Entry

Show students the proper way to write a bibliography entry using one of the trade books from your class library. Have students take out two of their textbooks. As a class, write a bibliography for one of the textbooks. Have each student write the bibliography for the other textbook. Ask a volunteer to write the bibliography on the board. Check to see that everyone writes it correctly. For homework, have students find five books in their homes and write the bibliography for each.

Example: Cushman, Karen. (1995). *The Midwife's Apprentice.* New York: Clarion Books.

Name _____

☆ Filmstrip Book Report ☆

For this book report, you will create a "film-strip" that tells about the book that you read. You will then present your filmstrip orally to the class.

☑ Check off each requirement after you've completed it.

Requirements

☐ PART ONE: RESEARCH

1. Pick a topic you're studying and find three books on the subject.
2. Show the books to your teacher for approval.
3. Your teacher will help you choose one book that must be read completely. The other two books will be used as reference books.
4. Review the graphic organizer before you start reading. As you read, fill out the organizer to help you plan your filmstrip.

☐ PART TWO: BLACK-AND-WHITE FILMSTRIP

1. Use the research from the books you read to design your filmstrip.
2. Use the templates provided to create a nine-panel filmstrip.
3. Use the information you entered in your graphic organizer to lay out each panel.
4. Your filmstrip should follow the guidelines listed below:

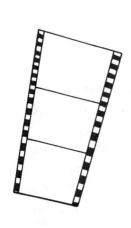

- **PANEL 1:** should include the title of your filmstrip, your name, and a general picture about the topic.

- **PANELS 2 to 5:** should include a four-panel history of your topic. Order the panels sequentially. Include two complete sentences describing the illustrations for each panel.

- **PANELS 6 & 7:** should include illustrations of famous people associated with your topic. Include two complete sentences describing the illustrations for each panel.

- **PANEL 8:** should illustrate an interesting fact about your topic that you did not include in an earlier panel. Include two complete sentences describing the illustration.

⊚ **PANEL 9:** should illustrate your thoughts about what the future holds in relation to your topic. Use your imagination when thinking about the possibilities. Include two complete sentences describing the illustration.

5. Use pencil to draw the filmstrip.

6. Then use a fine black marker to trace over the drawings.

7. Erase your pencil lines.

Make sure your pictures are clear and your printing is neat. If you have a typewriter or a computer, you should print out the text and glue it into the proper space for each panel.

☐ PART THREE: COLORED FILMSTRIP

Bring your black-and-white filmstrip to class. Your teacher will copy your filmstrip onto overhead transparencies.

⊛ Use *permanent* markers to color in the panels. Color the *back* of the panel so the black lines do not rub off.

⊛ When you have finished coloring in your filmstrip, cut out the three-panel strips and use clear tape to attach them in a long nine-panel strip.

☐ PART FOUR: ORAL PRESENTATION

You will use the overhead projector to present the filmstrip to the class.

1. Use a small index card for each panel, and write brief notes about the panel.

2. The information on the index cards should go into more detail than is included in the panel. You should use some of the information you wrote down on your graphic organizer.

3. On the last notecard, write a bibliography of the three books you used to do your research. You will turn in your notecards after your oral presentation.

4. As each panel of your filmstrip is shown on the overhead projector, discuss the information in the panel and use your notecards to elaborate on the details.

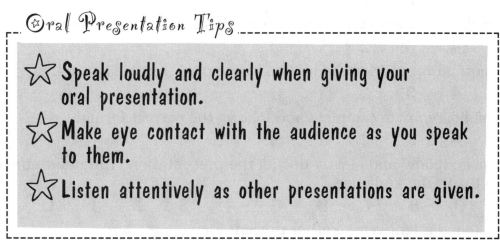

Oral Presentation Tips

☆ Speak loudly and clearly when giving your oral presentation.

☆ Make eye contact with the audience as you speak to them.

☆ Listen attentively as other presentations are given.

Name _____

Filmstrip Book Report R U B R I C

1. Panel 1 includes the title, your name, and a related illustration.

   5   4   3   2   1   0

2. Panels 2–5 present illustrations of important details related to your topic, and each panel includes two complete sentences.

Panel 2						Panel 3					
5	**4**	**3**	**2**	**1**	**0**	**5**	**4**	**3**	**2**	**1**	**0**
Panel 4						Panel 5					
5	**4**	**3**	**2**	**1**	**0**	**5**	**4**	**3**	**2**	**1**	**0**

3. Panels 6–7 include illustrations telling about famous people and two complete sentences describing each panel.

Panel 6						Panel 7					
5	**4**	**3**	**2**	**1**	**0**	**5**	**4**	**3**	**2**	**1**	**0**

4. Panel 8 illustrates an interesting fact about the topic and is described in two complete sentences.

   5   4   3   2   1   0

5. Panel 9 illustrates your thoughts about what the future holds in relation to the topic. You use two complete sentences to describe the illustration.

   5   4   3   2   1   0

6. Your pictures are executed carefully and creatively.

   10   9   8   7   6   5   4   3   2   1   0

7. Your pictures relate to the information in each panel.

   10   9   8   7   6   5   4   3   2   1   0

8. The writing is neat and legible.

   5   4   3   2   1   0

9. The spelling, punctuation, and grammar are correct.

   5   4   3   2   1   0

10. Your notecards are filled out well and were used during your oral presentation.

    5   4   3   2   1   0

11. Your bibliography is complete and follows the correct format.

    5   4   3   2   1   0

12. You spoke loudly and clearly during the presentation. You maintained eye contact with the audience.

    10   9   8   7   6   5   4   3   2   1   0

13. You listened attentively to other presentations.

    5   4   3   2   1   0

Name _____

Filmstrip Book Report   GRAPHIC ORGANIZER

PANELS 2-5

Fill out the graphic organizer. If relevant, include the dates in which major events occurred and notes about each event. Choose four of the events or details from the list below to include in your filmstrip.

DATE   **MAJOR EVENT OR BREAKTHROUGH THAT OCCURRED**

Notes < Who, What, Where, When, Why, How > : _____

_____

_____

Notes about the event: _____

_____

_____

Notes about the event: _____

_____

_____

Notes about the event: _____

_____

_____

Notes about the event: _____

_____

_____

Notes about the event: _____

_____

_____

Name _____

Filmstrip Book Report   GRAPHIC ORGANIZERS

PANELS 6-7

Write notes about three famous people associated with your topic. Choose two of them to include in your filmstrip.

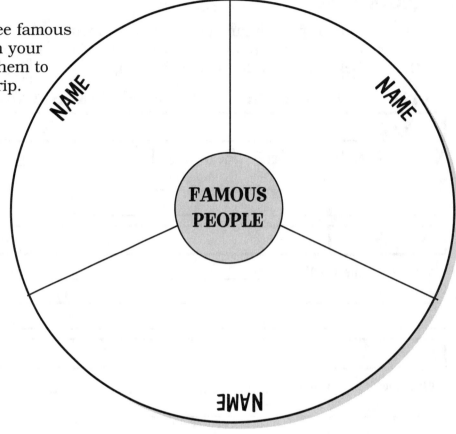

NAME

NAME

FAMOUS PEOPLE

NAME

PANEL 8

On the lines below write notes about interesting facts you learned while reading your book.

PANEL 9

On the lines below write your thoughts about what the future may hold regarding this topic.

	PAGE	

Name _____

Filmstrip Book Report TEMPLATE

Road-Map Book Report

NOTES TO THE TEACHER

Students Will Need Copies of:
⊙ requirements (pages 66–67)
⊙ rubric (page 68)
⊙ graphic organizers (page 69–70; two copies of each per student)

Important Tips:
Have markers, crayons, and paints on hand for students to use in creating their road maps. If possible, set out real road maps for kids to refer to and "borrow" from.

HOW TO USE THIS UNIT

1. First, review the requirements and the rubric with students.

2. Next, have students read their chosen books.

3. Have the students fill out their graphic organizers as they read their books. Check to see that they are on the right track.

4. Have students do preliminary sketches of their road maps prior to embarking on their final products.

5. For the final road map, suggest that students work in pencil first so they can make necessary changes. Later, they can go over their work in pen or marker.

Selecting Books

While this unit can be adapted to most genres of books, we have found that it works particularly well with historical nonfiction. We have students choose a book that is related to a particular period in history that we are studying in social studies. Focusing on one specific period makes it easier for us to help the students.

In order to help students pace themselves, set due dates for the following short-term goals:

1. Book should be read by: _____

2. Graphic organizers should be finished by: _____

3. Final draft is due by: _____

Breaking up the report into separate due dates helps less-organized students.

ACTIVITIES TO EXTEND LEARNING

A Map Center
Invite students to collect maps to create a map learning center. Encourage them to find all different kinds of maps: weather, transportation, land-use, population, as well as road maps. Display some of the maps on a bulletin board. Discuss the differences and similarities found on all the maps the class has collected. Be sure to point out and discuss features such as keys, scales, symbols, compass roses, and so on.

Classroom Cartographers
Encourage students to map your classroom, or even your school. Be sure they include a map key and a north arrow. They may want to create special symbols and use different colors for features such as desks, chairs, and closets. Display their finished maps in your classroom.

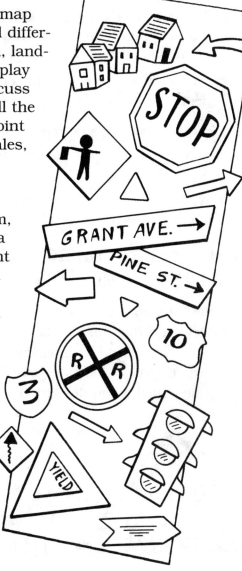

Name _____

☆ Road-Map Book Report ☆

For this book report you will create a time-line in the shape of a road map. The road map will show important events from a particular period in history covered in your book in sequential order.

✔ Check off each requirement after you've completed it.

Requirements

☐ PART ONE: GRAPHIC ORGANIZER 1

Read a historical nonfiction book that is about a specific period in history. As you read your book, take notes on graphic organizer 1.

- ◉ Include major events that took place, important dates, pertinent people, and details.

☐ PART TWO: GRAPHIC ORGANIZER 2

On graphic organizer 2, put the events from graphic organizer 1 into sequential order.

- ◉ Write two complete sentences for each event, using your information from graphic organizer 1.

☐ PART THREE: DESIGNING YOUR ROAD MAP

◉ DESIGNING THE ROAD

1. Use a piece of white construction paper (12 x 18 inches).
2. Design a road on this paper that has a beginning and an end.
3. This road could be a winding country road, a busy downtown street, a superhighway, or a design of your choice.
4. Use pencil when designing your road in case you need to make changes.

◎ DESIGNING THE STOPS

Once you have designed your road, add ten "stops" along the way. These stops can be:

◎ traffic lights	◎ exit ramps
◎ stop signs	◎ detours
◎ yield signs	◎ toll booths
◎ street names	◎ road hazards
◎ bridges	◎ stores and buildings

◎ ADDING THE INFORMATION

1. At each stop (starting with stop 1) write the title and date of event 1 from graphic organizer 2.
2. Under the title write the two complete sentences that accompany that particular event.
3. Continue along your stops, adding events in sequential order as you move along the road.
4. Make sure you have clearly marked a beginning and an end to your road map.
5. Add small icons (pictures) next to each stop that relate to that event.

◎ FINISHING TOUCHES

1. Create a title for your road map (e.g., Road Map to the Revolutionary War). Use creative lettering.
2. Add landscaping to your design to fill up empty spaces.
3. Color all pictures, roads, landscaping, and your title.
4. Use a fine black marker to trace over all writing.
5. Erase all pencil lines.

Name _____

Road-Map Book Report R U B R I C ☆

1. Graphic organizers 1 and 2 are completely filled out according to the directions given.

   10   9   8   7   6   5   4   3   2   1   0

2. The ten events relate to the time period your book covered and are in sequential order.

   10   9   8   7   6   5   4   3   2   1   0

3. The ten events are the most important in the particular time period your book covered.

   10   9   8   7   6   5   4   3   2   1   0

4. Two complete, detailed sentences describe each event.

   10   9   8   7   6   5   4   3   2   1   0

5. The information describing each event is important.

   10   9   8   7   6   5   4   3   2   1   0

6. The information describing each event is accurate.

   10   9   8   7   6   5   4   3   2   1   0

7. Spelling, punctuation, and grammar are correct.

   10   9   8   7   6   5   4   3   2   1   0

8. The icons (pictures) relate to each event and are creatively illustrated.

   10   9   8   7   6   5   4   3   2   1   0

9. Visual presentation is creative and neat (writing, title, use of all the space provided).

   10   9   8   7   6   5   4   3   2   1   0

10. The design of your road map is unique and well planned. The stops are creatively displayed.

    10   9   8   7   6   5   4   3   2   1   0

Name _____

Road-Map Book Report GRAPHIC ORGANIZER

GRAPHIC ORGANIZER 1

Take notes as you read your book. Write down important events and details that relate to the historical period your book covers. You will need two of these sheets.

☆ EVENT ☆	DATE	DETAILS	☆ KEY PEOPLE ☆

Name _____

Road-Map Book Report GRAPHIC ORGANIZER

GRAPHIC ORGANIZER 2

Choose ten major events from graphic organizer #1 to fill out the information below. List the events in sequential order. You will need two of these sheets.

MAJOR EVENT	DATE	TWO COMPLETE SENTENCES
Number: ___		
Number: ___		
Number: ___		
Number: ___		
Number: ___		

Tri-Fold Book Report

NOTES TO THE TEACHER

Students Will Need Copies of:
- requirements (pages 73–74)
- rubric (page 75)
- graphic organizers pages 76–78)

Important Tips:
Pre-made tri-fold cardboard displays are available at most office supply stores. You can also make a display by folding a large piece of cardboard (about 3 feet high x 4.5 feet wide) into thirds.

HOW TO USE THIS UNIT

1. First, review the requirements and the rubric with the students.

2. Next, have the students read their chosen books and do the research.

3. Then, have the students fill out their graphic organizers. You may have them complete individual sections of the graphic organizers for homework. Check to see that they are on the right track.

4. Finally, check the students' rough drafts for the writing sections of this project at least one week before the final project is due.

Selecting Books

We use this unit to integrate the fine arts into our reading program. Our students are invited to choose a famous artist or architect to research and report on. With some adaption of the requirements, you could have your students choose a sculptor, photographer, or another type of craftsperson.

In order to help students pace themselves, set due dates for the following short-term goals:

1. Research/timelines should be finished by: _____
2. Graphic organizer should be finished by: _____
3. Rough draft is due by: _____
4. Final draft is due by: _____

Setting separate "mini" due dates for the graphic organizers and their accompanying rough drafts will help less-organized students.

ACTIVITIES TO EXTEND LEARNING

Personal Timelines
Have your students create a timeline of their life. As a class brainstorm a variety of formats that the students could use for the timeline, or select a specific one that you want them to use. The students should brainstorm a list of important events in their life and then put the events in chronological order.

As a homework assignment have the students create a timeline using this information. They should have at least 15 events listed. Be sure to discuss as a class the different timelines that the students created.

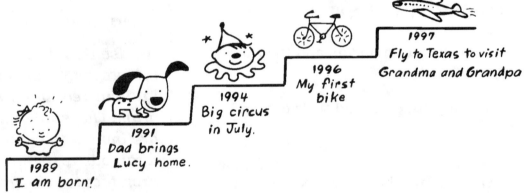

Art Appreciation
If possible, have your school's art teacher or a knowledgeable parent come into your classroom to conduct a lesson on art appreciation. He or she could introduce the students to a variety of artists or artistic styles. Discuss Impressionism with the students. Tell them that Monet would often draw while in a boat. He would paint the reflections he saw on the water. Invite students to make their own "Impressionistic" art. Tell them to fold a piece of paper in half. They should use colored chalk to draw a picture on the top half. Then they should wet the bottom half and refold the paper. Have them separate the two halves, and leave the paper open to dry.

Name _____

☆ Tri-Fold Book Report ☆

This report is a research project on the life and works of a famous artist. You will gather information about this artist from various sources and present the information on a tri-fold display board.

☑ Check off each requirement after you've completed it.

Requirements

☐ PART ONE: RESEARCH

Pick an artist whose life and work you would like to research. Find five reference books or articles on the artist. At least one of your resources should be a library book.

Some suggested references include:

- ◉ library books
- ◉ encyclopedias
- ◉ newspaper and magazine articles
- ◉ Internet articles

1. Show the reference books and articles to your teacher for approval.
2. Review the graphic organizers before you start reading. As you read, fill out the organizers to help you plan your project.

PART TWO: PROJECT ELEMENTS

☐ **PROJECT TITLE:** Use creative lettering to write the artist's name on the top of the center panel. Make it eye-catching and colorful. Write your name below the artist's.

☐ **TIMELINE:** Design a timeline of your artist's life that includes at least 15 events, such as:

Personal Life	Artistic Life
◉ birth	◉ awards
◉ early life	◉ education
◉ marriage/children	◉ when major works were created
◉ death	◉ major artistic periods

Create a rough draft of your timeline by listing the events from your graphic organizer in chronological order. Place the timeline of the artist's life at the top of the left-hand panel. (See illustration on the next page.)

☐ **BIOGRAPHY:** Use the timeline information to write a biography of the artist.

1. One paragraph should be about his or her early life.
2. One paragraph should be about major events in his or her personal life.
3. At least two paragraphs should be about major events in the artist's life.
4. The biography should be either typed or neatly written.
5. Place this biography underneath the timeline. (See illustration.)

☐ **REPRODUCTION OF ARTIST'S WORK:** Choose one of the artist's major works and reproduce it so it looks as much like the original as possible. If the artist was a painter, you can choose to either draw or paint your picture.

1. The reproduction should be approximately one third the size of a panel.
2. Place this picture on the top of the right-hand panel. (See illustration.)
3. On an index card write a paragraph describing why this work was significant, what medium the artist used to create it, and when it was completed.
4. Place this index card underneath the reproduction.

☐ **DESIGNING YOUR OWN WORK:** Many artists are influenced by other artists. Study the style of your artist and create a new picture keeping that style in mind.

1. This picture should be approximately one third the size of a panel.
2. Place this drawing on the bottom of the right-hand panel.

☐ **LETTER TO THE ARTIST:** Write a letter to the artist describing what you like and dislike about his or her style and work. Think about the artist's color choices, subject matter, composition, and use of line, light, shape, texture, and shading.

1. This letter should be two paragraphs long. One paragraph should focus on the elements you like, and one should focus on the elements you dislike.
2. Place this letter underneath the title on the center panel. (See illustration.)

☐ **RESPONSES TO ARTWORK:** Show 10 people of different ages a color copy of the picture you chose to reproduce.

1. Ask each person to describe the picture. Summarize each person's response in a complete sentence.
2. Write or type these responses; label them "A Picture Is Worth a Thousand Words."
3. Place this next to the letter you wrote to the artist.

☐ **BIBLIOGRAPHY:** On an index card, write a bibliography of the five reference books you used.

1. Your books should be listed in alphabetical order by the author's last name.
2. Place this bibliography on the bottom of the center panel.

Name _____

Tri-Fold Book Report RUBRIC

1. The artist's name is creatively written. Your name is included.

   5   4   3   2   1   0

2. The timeline includes at least 15 significant events from the artist's personal and artistic life. They were listed in chronological order.

   10   9   8   7   6   5   4   3   2   1   0

3. The biography consists of at least four well-developed paragraphs. It follows the format listed.

   15   14   13   12   11   10   9   8   7   6   5   4   3   2   1   0

4. The reproduction of your artist's work is carefully and creatively executed. The artist's style is evident.

   10   9   8   7   6   5   4   3   2   1   0

5. The paragraph describing the reproduction is well written and explains the significance of this work, the medium used, and the date it was created.

   5   4   3   2   1   0

6. The picture you drew imitates the artist's style and is carefully and creatively executed.

   10   9   8   7   6   5   4   3   2   1   0

7. The letter to the artist includes at least two thoughtful paragraphs and describes what you liked and disliked about the artist's style and work.

   10   9   8   7   6   5   4   3   2   1   0

8. The 10 responses to the artwork are written in complete sentences and the title is included.

   10   9   8   7   6   5   4   3   2   1   0

9. The bibliography is completed accurately and includes five references.

   5   4   3   2   1   0

10. Spelling, grammar, and punctuation are correct.

    10   9   8   7   6   5   4   3   2   1   0

11. The overall presentation is creative, well organized, and neatly written or typed.

    10   9   8   7   6   5   4   3   2   1   0

Name _____

Tri-Fold Book Report GRAPHIC ORGANIZER

TIMELINE/BIOGRAPHY

Use note form (fragmented sentences) to fill out the graphic organizer. Use the information to help you with your timeline and biography. After you've completed the graphic organizer, list the events in chronological order before starting your time line.

MAJOR WORKS

Date:

Date:

Date:

Date:

Date:

ARTISTIC PERIOD

Date:

Date:

Date:

Date:

Date:

EDUCATION

Date:

Date:

Date:

MARRIAGE< S >

Date(s):

Spouse(s):

TIMELINE/ BIOGRAPHY ☆ FOR ☆

_____

_____

BIRTH

When:

Where:

DEATH

When:

Where:

How:

EARLY LIFE

Date:

Date:

Date:

Date:

AWARDS

Date:

Date:

Date:

Date:

INTERESTING FACTS

Date:

Date:

Date:

Date:

CHILDREN/FAMILY

Date:

Date:

Date:

Date:

Name _____

Tri-Fold Book Report   GRAPHIC ORGANIZERS

LETTER TO THE ARTIST

Brainstorm things you like and dislike about your artist's style and work. Use these notes to help you write a letter to your artist.

LIKE	DISLIKE

RESPONSES TO ARTWORK

Use the lines below to take notes on how the 10 people you interviewed responded to the artist's work.

NAME	AGE	RESPONSE
1		
2		
3		
4		
5		
6		
7		
8		
9		
10		

Name _____

Tri-Fold Book Report GRAPHIC ORGANIZER

BIBLIOGRAPHY

Use the following format to help you write down the necessary information for your bibliography. Be aware of the punctuation that is used. Remember to list your references in alphabetical order based on the author's last name.

1. _____ , _____ . (_____).
   Author's last name   Author's first name   Copyright date

   _____ . _____ : _____ .
   Title of book underlined   City published   Publisher

2. _____ , _____ . (_____).
   Author's last name   Author's first name   Copyright date

   _____ . _____ : _____ .
   Title of book underlined   City published   Publisher

3. _____ , _____ . (_____).
   Author's last name   Author's first name   Copyright date

   _____ . _____ : _____ .
   Title of book underlined   City published   Publisher

4. _____ , _____ . (_____).
   Author's last name   Author's first name   Copyright date

   _____ . _____ : _____ .
   Title of book underlined   City published   Publisher

5. _____ , _____ . (_____).
   Author's last name   Author's first name   Copyright date

   _____ . _____ : _____ .
   Title of book underlined   City published   Publisher

6. _____ , _____ . (_____).
   Author's last name   Author's first name   Copyright date

   _____ . _____ : _____ .
   Title of book underlined   City published   Publisher

Book Jacket Report

Students Will Need Copies of:
◉ requirements (pages 81–82)
◉ rubric (page 83)
◉ graphic organizers (pages 84–85)
◉ templates (pages 86–90)

Important Tips:
Each student will need a piece of oaktag, 11 inches high by 2 feet long. Be sure to have markers, crayons, and an array of art supplies on hand for students to use.

HOW TO USE THIS UNIT

1. First, review the requirements and the rubric with the students. The "Main Ideas Template" allows for nine chapters. If any student is reading a book that is longer than nine chapters, you can either have them combine chapters together or have them attach a second template over the first one.

2. Next, as a class, have students construct their book jackets.

3. Then, have students read their chosen books.

4. Next, have the students fill out their graphic organizers. You may have them complete individual sections of the graphic organizers for homework. Check to see that they are on the right track.

Selecting Books

The Book Jacket Report works well with all fiction books. (We allow students to choose any book they like.) However, this project can easily be adapted to be used with nonfiction books or books on particular genres such as mysteries, historical fiction, biographies, or autobiographies.

5. Finally, check students' rough drafts for the writing sections of this project at least one week before the final project is due.

--- *Suggested Due Dates* --

In order to help students pace themselves, set due dates for the following short-term goals:

1. Book should be read by: _____
2. Graphic organizers should be finished by: _____
3. Rough draft is due by: _____
4. Final draft is due by: _____

Setting separate "mini" due dates for the graphic organizers and their accompanying rough drafts will help less-organized students.

ACTIVITIES TO EXTEND LEARNING

Book Talk
Select several books from your library that have good examples of book jackets. Preview the book jackets with your class and discuss the following elements:

- the cover's layout and design
- the location of the publisher's name
- the author's note (short biography/picture)
- the paragraph on the back of the book that "sells" the book
- the reviews from magazines, newspapers, and other authors
- the summary of the book on the inside flap

During your book talk, you may also want to focus on the difference between the "sell" paragraph and the reviews. Discuss how the comments of a reviewer reflect one person's opinion of the book and how the "sell" is a short, factual paragraph explaining the highlights of the book.

Read a short picture book to the class. Have students write a one-sentence review of the book that expresses their opinion. Then, have students write one sentence that highlights the major event in the book. Share and discuss students' responses.

Language Review
A focus of this book report project is how students use adjectives and compound sentences. Review how adjectives are used to describe character traits. Show students how to use a thesaurus to find uncommon, vivid adjectives. Review the use of compound sentences as a tool for developing more elaborate and detailed sentences.

Name _____

☆ Book Jacket Report ☆

For this book report, you will create a book jacket that tells about the book you've chosen to read as well as the book's author.

☑ Check off each requirement after you've completed it.

Requirements

☐ **CONSTRUCTING THE BOOK JACKET**

To construct the jacket for the book you read, use a large sheet of oaktag.

1. Cut a sheet of oaktag 11 inches high by 2 feet long.
2. From the left side, measure in 4 inches and place a light pencil mark.
3. Also place a mark 11 inches from the left side.
4. Repeat steps 2–3 three times down the paper.
5. With a ruler and a pencil, lightly draw a line along the 4-inch marks and the 11-inch marks.
6. Follow steps 2–5 measuring from the right side of the paper. Your oaktag should now look like the illustration below.

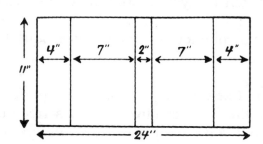

7. Fold the paper inward along the 4-inch guidelines.
8. Fold the paper inward along the 11-inch guidelines so that it looks like a book jacket. It should now look like the illustration above, at the right.
9. Open up the book jacket and place it in front of you so that the outside of the book jacket is facing up.
10. Starting from the left, lightly number the panels 1–5.
11. Turn the book jacket over. Starting from the left, lightly number the panels 6–10. You are now ready to start creating the panels for your book jacket.

CONSTRUCTING THE PANELS

When creating the panels for your book jacket, you should use the corresponding templates, then glue them into place with a glue stick.

☐ **COVER/PANEL 4:** Design a cover for your book jacket that includes the title of the book, the author's name, and your name. Include a related illustration.

☐ **SPINE/PANEL 3:** Use creative lettering to design a spine for your book jacket. Include the title of the book and the author's name. Write the name of the publisher at the bottom of the panel.

☐ **BACK COVER/PANEL 2:** On the top half of panel 2 write a paragraph that highlights the most exciting element of the book. This paragraph should make the reader want to read the book but should not include your personal opinion. On the bottom half of panel 2 write a one-paragraph review of the book. This paragraph should tell what you liked and disliked about the book.

☐ **AUTHOR'S NOTES/PANEL 1:** On the top half of panel 1, glue a photo of yourself or draw a self-portrait. Underneath your picture write a one-paragraph biography about yourself. Consider the following when writing your biography.

- ◉ important dates   ◉ education   ◉ activities
- ◉ interests/hobbies   ◉ family   ◉ place of residence

☐ **SUMMARY/PANELS 5 AND 6:** Beginning on panel 5 and continuing on panel 6, write a three-paragraph summary of the book that highlights the beginning, middle, and end of the novel. Each paragraph should include at least two compound or complex sentences (a total of six sentences); you should underline these sentences.

☐ **MAIN IDEAS/PANEL 7:** Write a complete sentence describing the main ideas for each of the chapters in the novel.

☐ **MAIN CHARACTER/PANEL 8:** Use creative lettering to write the name of the main character. Use a thesaurus to find five adjectives that describe him or her. These adjectives should be words that you do not use in your everyday vocabulary. For example, don't use words like *nice, happy,* or *pretty* to describe the character.

☐ **PROBLEM-SOLUTION/PANEL 9:** Choose three problems that occurred in your book, and draw a picture that illustrates each of them. Under each picture, write a complete sentence describing the problem. Then, draw pictures of the solution(s) to each of the problems and write complete sentences describing them. The pictures should be creative, colorful, and carefully drawn.

☐ **VOCABULARY/PANEL 10:** As you read your book, look up words whose meanings you don't know. List alphabetically 10 words and their definitions that were unfamiliar to you when you first read the book.

Name _____

Book Jacket Report R U B R I C

1. The cover of your book jacket includes your name, the author's name, and the book's title. The illustration is creatively designed and relates to the book's theme.
   10   9   8   7   6   5   4   3   2   1   0

2. The spine of your book jacket includes the title of the novel, the author's name, and the publisher. The title is written in creative lettering.
   5   4   3   2   1   0

3. The highlights of your book are written in a well-developed paragraph and make the reader want to read your book. You do not include your personal opinion.
   5   4   3   2   1   0

4. Your review of your book is written in a well-developed paragraph and gives specific examples as to why you liked or disliked the novel.
   5   4   3   2   1   0

5. The author's notes include either a photo of yourself or a self-portrait. Your biography is written in a complete, well-developed paragraph.
   10   9   8   7   6   5   4   3   2   1   0

6. The summary includes three well-developed paragraphs that highlight the beginning, middle, and end of the novel.
   10   9   8   7   6   5   4   3   2   1   0

7. Each paragraph in your summary includes at least two compound or complex sentences. These sentences are underlined.
   10   9   8   7   6   5   4   3   2   1   0

8. A complete sentence accurately describes the main idea for each chapter.
   5   4   3   2   1   0

9. The name of the main character is written in creative lettering and five vivid adjectives describe the main character.
   5   4   3   2   1   0

10. The pictures of the problems and solutions are carefully drawn. A complete sentence describes each picture.
    10   9   8   7   6   5   4   3   2   1   0

11. Ten unfamiliar words are listed alphabetically and defined.
    5   4   3   2   1   0

12. Spelling, grammar, and punctuation are correct.
    10   9   8   7   6   5   4   3   2   1   0

13. The overall presentation is creative and well organized. You have written neatly in ink and in script, using your best handwriting.
    10   9   8   7   6   5   4   3   2   1   0

Name _____

Book Jacket Report GRAPHIC ORGANIZERS

SUMMARY

Use note form (fragmented sentences) to fill out the graphic organizer. List ten elements from each section of the book—the beginning, middle, and end. Use this information to help you write your summary.

◎ BEGINNING ◎
1
2
3
4
5
6
7
8
9
10

◎ MIDDLE ◎
1
2
3
4
5
6
7
8
9
10

◎ ENDING ◎
1
2
3
4
5
6
7
8
9
10

BACK COVER/HIGHLIGHTS

Think about three major highlights from the book. In the space to the left, write one word that describes the highlight. In the space to the right, write notes that explain what happened.

HIGHLIGHT	☆ Explanation of Highlight ☆

HIGHLIGHT	☆ Explanation of Highlight ☆

Name _____

Book Jacket Report GRAPHIC ORGANIZERS

BACK COVER/HIGHLIGHTS (CONTINUED)

HIGHLIGHT	☆ Explanation of Highlight ☆

BACK COVER/REVIEW

Use this graphic organizer to help you plan your review of the book. In each oval write a word that describes an element of the book that you either liked or disliked (plot, characterization, writing style, interest level, etc.) In the boxes write notes describing what you liked and/or disliked about each of these elements.

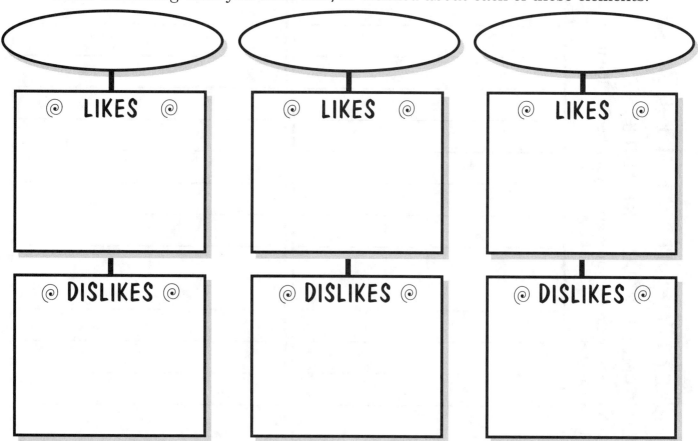

MAIN IDEA

As you read your novel, use a sheet of paper to write notes about the main ideas of each chapter. Write the notes immediately after you finish reading the chapter.

Book Jacket Report TEMPLATE

SUMMARY TEMPLATE/PANELS 5 AND 6

Use this template to write the summary of your book. Glue the first part of your summary onto panel 5, and continue it on panel 6.

Book Jacket Report TEMPLATE

BACK COVER/PANEL 2

Use the top half of this template to write the paragraph that highlights the most exciting elements of the book.
Use the bottom half of this panel to write the one-paragraph review of the book.

Book Jacket Report TEMPLATE

MAIN IDEAS/ PANEL 7

Use this template to write the main ideas for each of the chapters in your book. Write the chapter number on the bold line and the main idea after it.

Chapter _____ :

Chapter _____ :

Chapter _____ :

Chapter _____ :

Chapter _____ :

Chapter _____ :

Chapter _____ :

Chapter _____ :

Chapter _____ :

Chapter _____ :

Book Jacket Report TEMPLATE

PROBLEM-SOLUTION/PANEL 9

Use this template to draw pictures illustrating three of the problems/solutions that occurred in the book. On the lines below each picture, write a complete sentence describing the problem and its solution(s).

☆ PROBLEMS ☆   ☆ SOLUTIONS ☆

Book Jacket Report TEMPLATE

AUTHOR'S NOTES TEMPLATE/ PANEL 1—AND VOCABULARY TEMPLATE/PANEL 10

Use the template on the left to draw your self-portrait and write the author's notes paragraph. Use the template on the right to alphabetically list and define the 10 unfamiliar words you found.

VOCABULARY

1
2
3
4
5
6
7
8
9
10

Pop-Up Book Report

Students Will Need Copies of:
- requirements (pages 93–95)
- rubric (page 96)

Important Tips:
Students will each need six sheets of construction paper (8.5 x 14 inches allows for more writing space). Have color construction paper, markers, crayons, scissors, and an array of craft materials available for students.

HOW TO USE THIS UNIT

1. First, review the requirements and the rubric with students.

2. Next, demonstrate the process of creating a pop-up page. (See detailed directions on student pages 93–95.) Tip: you may want to construct a pop-up yourself so your students will have a model to refer to.

3. Then, have the students read their chosen books.

4. Finally, check students' rough drafts for the writing sections of this project, using the suggested due dates on the following page.

Selecting Books

The Pop-Up Book Report works especially well with all fiction books. (We allow our students to choose any book they wish.) However, this project can easily be adapted for any genre including science fiction, historical fiction, mysteries, biography, myths, tall tales, and folktales.

In order to help students pace themselves, set due dates for the following short-term goals:

1. Book should be read by: _____
2. Summary rough draft is due by: _____
3. Problem-solution rough draft is due by: _____
4. Setting rough draft is due by: _____
5. Alternate setting draft is due by: _____
6. Character-study roughdraft is due by: _____

Setting separate "mini" due dates for the final draft of each page will help less-organized students.

ACTIVITIES TO EXTEND LEARNING

Venn Diagram

Review the use of a Venn Diagram as a tool to compare and contrast two or more things. On the board, draw a three-way Venn diagram. Put the names of three students above the circles. As a class, brainstorm the differences and similarities of the three students. Discuss with your students where these differences and similarities would be placed within the Venn diagram.

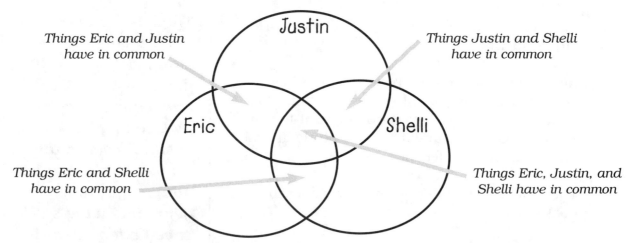

Exploring the Setting

Read a picture book that has a rich, distinctive setting. After reading it, discuss the setting of the book with the class. Brainstorm a list of alternate settings in which the story could have been set. Discuss how these alternate settings would influence the events in the story and possibly change its outcome.

Name _____

☆ Pop-Up Book Report ☆

For this book report, you will tell about a book you've chosen to read by creating a pop-up scene. Your report will include a summary, and information about the book's characters, setting, and problem and solution.

☑ Check off each requirement after you've completed it.

Requirements

☐ **CONSTRUCTING THE POP-UP BOOK**

    1. Draw a rough sketch of the scene you want to create and decide which elements will "pop up."

    2. Fold a piece of construction paper in half widthwise.

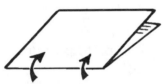

    3. Along the folded edge, cut two slits of equal length for each of the pop-up tabs in your scene.

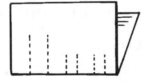

    4. Open the paper up, and gently pull each of pop-up tabs forward.

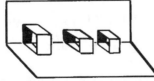

    5. Fold the paper again so that each of the pop-up tabs falls into the center. Press the base of each tab so that it forms a crease.

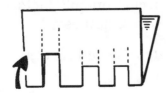

6. Open your paper up and illustrate the background of your scene.

7. Draw the pop-up elements of your scene, and glue them onto the front of each tab.

8. Use a ruler and pencil to *lightly* draw guide-lines on the paper in from of your pop-up scene. Write the paragraph in pencil first. Then trace over it using a thin black marker. Finally, erase the guidelines and pencil marks.

TABS

9. Repeat these steps for each page of your book. Put your pages in order, one on top of the other. Glue the bottom of one page to the top of the next, until all of the pages are joined. Use glue stick rather than glue so that the paper doesn't buckle.

10. Get another sheet of construction paper and fold it in half. Use creative lettering to write the name of the book you read, the author's name, and the words "Pop-up Book by [your name]." Include a related illustration. Put the pop-up pages in the folded cover, and glue the cover into place.

CREATING THE PAGES

☐ **SUMMARY/PAGE ONE:** Write a complete paragraph that gives a brief summary of the book. Include the following

- ◉ author   ◉ main character   ◉ conclusion
- ◉ title   ◉ major events

Create a pop-up picture that illustrates your favorite scene from the book.

☐ **PROBLEM-SOLUTION/PAGE TWO:** Write a complete paragraph that describes the main problem and solution of the story. Divide the page for your picture vertically. Write PROBLEM at the top of the left panel and SOLUTION at the top of the right panel.

1. On the left panel create a pop-up picture that illustrates the problem.

2. On the right panel create a pop-up picture that illustrates the solution.

☐ **SETTING/PAGE THREE:** Write a complete paragraph that describes the setting of the book. Consider the following:

- ◉ time period   ◉ socioeconomic factors   ◉ climate
- ◉ geographical location   ◉ surroundings   ◉ season

Create a pop-up picture that illustrates the setting of the book.

☐ **ALTERNATE SETTING/PAGE FOUR:** Choose an alternate setting for your book. Write a complete paragraph that describes the alternate setting and how it would change the outcome of the story. Create a pop-up picture that illustrates the alternate setting of the book.

☐ **CHARACTER STUDY/PAGE FIVE:** Use the Venn diagram below to compare and contrast the main character, a secondary character, and yourself. Be sure to fill in all the spaces provided. Copy this Venn diagram and the information onto the bottom of your fifth page. Choose one of the main differences between you and the main character from your Venn diagram.

 1. Divide the page for your picture vertically.

 2. Write the name of the main character on the top of the left panel and your name on the top of the right panel.

 3. On the left panel create a pop-up of the main character in a scene illustrating the difference you chose from your Venn diagram.

 4. On the right panel create a pop-up of yourself in a scene illustrating the difference.

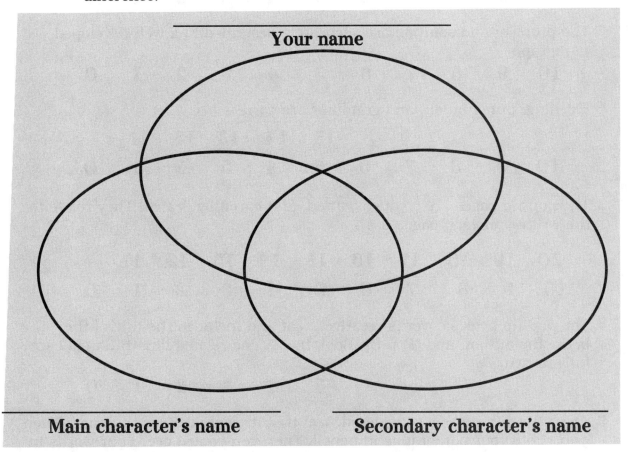

Your name

Main character's name   **Secondary character's name**

☐ **COVER:** Design a cover for your book that includes the title of the book, the author, and the words "Pop-up Book by [your name]." Include a related illustration.

Name _____

Pop-Up Book Report R U B R I C

1. Your summary is written in a well-developed paragraph and includes a brief description of the main character, major events, title, author, and conclusion.

      10   9   8   7   6   5   4   3   2   1   0

2. The Venn diagram is complete and accurately filled out with thoughtful responses.

      10   9   8   7   6   5   4   3   2   1   0

3. The setting of the book is described in a well-developed paragraph.

      10   9   8   7   6   5   4   3   2   1   0

4. The alternate setting is described in a well-developed paragraph. You explain how it would change the outcome of the story.

      10   9   8   7   6   5   4   3   2   1   0

5. The problem and solution are accurately described in a well-developed paragraph.

      10   9   8   7   6   5   4   3   2   1   0

6. Spelling, punctuation, and grammar are correct.

                              15   14   13   12   11
      10   9   8   7   6   5   4   3   2   1   0

7. The pop-up pages are creative, varied, and carefully drawn. They relate to the writing on each page.

      20   19   18   17   16   15   14   13   12   11
      10   9   8   7   6   5   4   3   2   1   0

8. The pop-up book's cover is creative, neat and includes the title of the book, the author, and "Pop-Up Book by…". The related illustration is carefully drawn.

                              5   4   3   2   1   0

9. Overall neatness was considered. You first drew guidelines in pencil. Then you wrote your paragraphs in pencil. Then you copied over your words in pen or marker. And, finally, you erased your guidelines and pencil marks.

      10   9   8   7   6   5   4   3   2   1   0